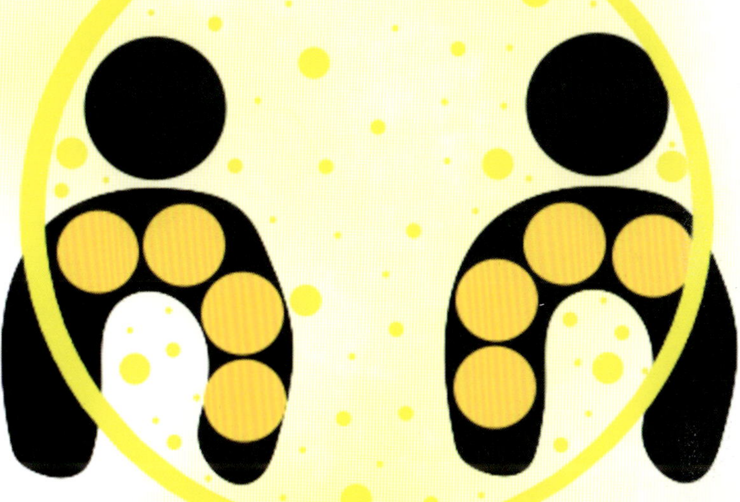

Hi, my name is Krystal Randall. My Mum is a Yaegl woman and my Dad is a Bundjalung man. I grew up with my family in a small Aboriginal community about an hour from Grafton. It's located in the BEAUTIFUL Northern Rivers area of New South Wales.

beautiful

I had a very happy childhood with my FAMILY and friends. One of my fondest memories is when we would spend time with our Pop on the weekends in nature. He would teach us many things about the bush. He knew so much about flora and fauna. We loved and cherished the time we spent with him.

family

I learned so much from the time I spent with my family. One of the most important things I learned is how to talk about and SHARE my feelings with others.
Communicating with others is not always easy but it's really important.
This is why I came up with the idea of my Yarn Circles Wellbeing Cards.

sharing

I use my Yarn Cards in traditional Yarning Circles. It helps those students who really don't feel like talking about their feelings. They can choose a card that describes their feelings, like this SCARED card. We can then talk about ways to help them move past the bad feelings and focus on the good ones. These cards help them to heal.

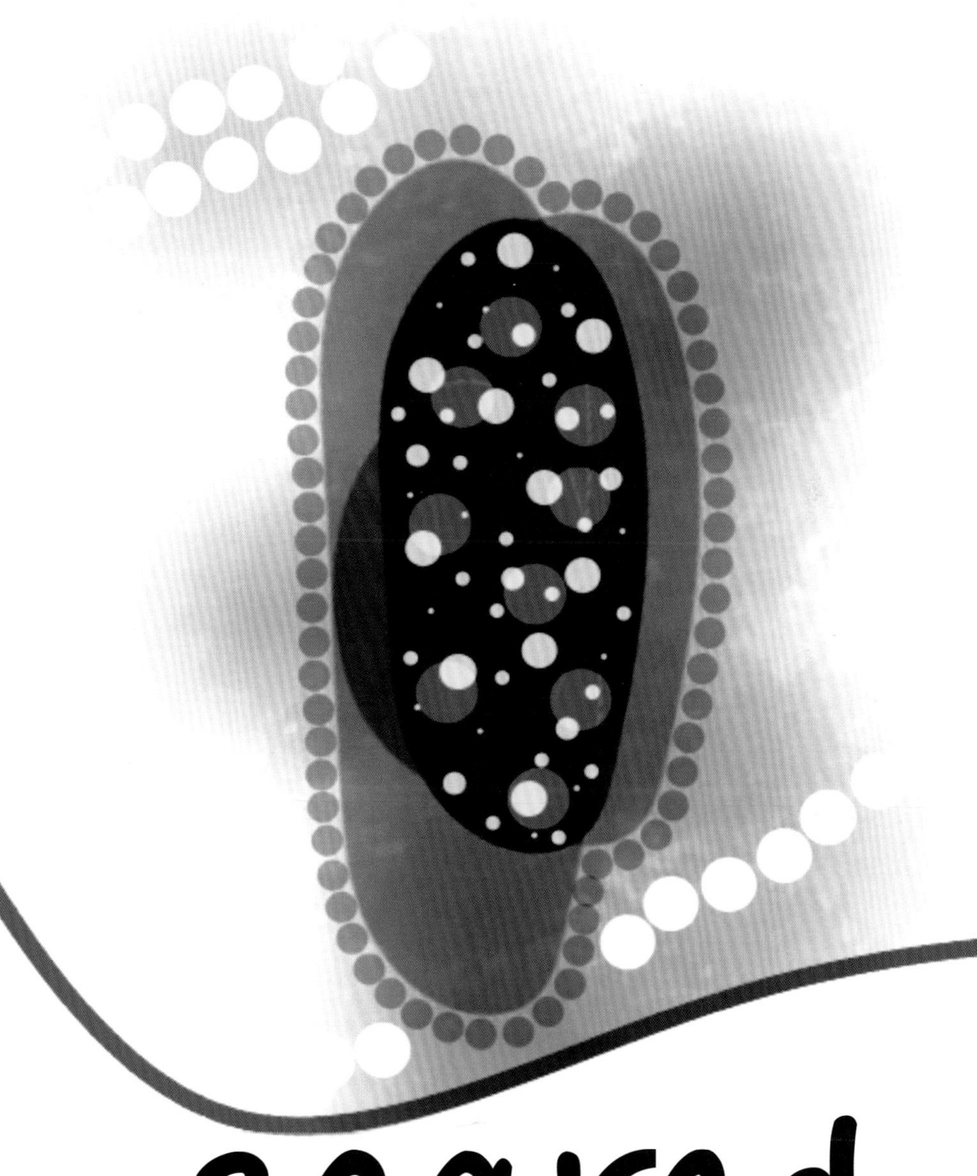

scared

Sometimes it can be hard to let go of something bad that's happened. Many of our ancestors experienced very difficult times. Even today, it's hard for some Indigenous people to forgive others for things that happened in the past.
Unfortunately, these events can't be changed. But what we can do is to let go of the HURT and anger and focus on a brighter future.

hurt

One of the ways we can stop these bad feelings is by focusing on all the good things that make you happy. These can include your family, your FRIENDSHIPS, your pets, your hobbies, and even nature. What other positive things can you think of that can make you happy?

friendship

When you wake up every day and feel grateful for what you have, it makes you feel good. It helps you to be more thankful for your life and the important people in it. Writing a gratitude journal is a great way of recording your thoughts and feelings. It helps to remind you of how lucky and LOVED you really are!

love

Have you ever noticed how you feel after being KIND to someone? It makes you feel good too! It's like a gift that keeps on giving. Even something as small as a smile or a hug can be enough to make someone feel better.

kind

When we dwell on something bad that's happened, we sometimes get ANGRY and make the problem seem bigger in our minds. These negative thoughts can make our body sick. This is called stress. We need to stop dwelling on these problems so they won't dwell on us!

angry

Another way that you can be positive is to figure out your goals in life and work towards trying to achieve them. They can be small goals like going for a walk in nature every day. Or they can be bigger goals like working out what career you'd like to have when you're older. Whatever your goals, big or small, always be STRONG enough to stick with them.

strong

And remember, being HAPPY is a choice that you can make for yourself. You can choose to be sad, or angry, or resentful, and feel all the bad feelings that come with these emotions. Or you can choose to be HAPPY and enjoy all the wonderful feelings that come with being HAPPY. It's up to you!

happy

Word bank

Yaegl
Bundjalung
Aboriginal
community
Grafton
beautiful
Northern
fondest
flora
fauna
cherished
important
communicating
wellbeing
traditional
describes
ancestors
experienced
difficult
unfortunately
events
dwell
negative
positive
grateful
gratitude
journal
noticed
figure
achieve
remember
resentful
emotions
career
wonderful